ESHWARI

KANISETTY LAKSHMI HARIKA

DEDICATED TO,

*MY READERS WHO FEELS MANY
CHARACTERS IN STORIES,*

*WHO NEVER READS CANNOT
EXPERIENCE THE WAY OF LIFE.*

ॐ

Contents

FOREWORD

As one of the readers, I am sharing my personal experience after reading the story of **"ESHWARI"** .It resonated deeply with my own life. The dark truths that revealed from Eshwari's family the struggles, expectations and the harsh realities that women often face.

This story questions the nature of justice whether seeking revenge truly brings closure.This story was the personal reminder of the strengths of a mother's love and the unyielding spirit that refuses to be in silence.

We are living in a society where ancient traditions and modern belief's clash,unfolds the haunting story of **"ESHWARI"** a mother whose life is torn apart by a forced decision she has nothing in her hands neither control nor accept it.

Eshwari an unborn child, a girl fated to bring joy,is cruelly taken from her by a merciless abortion which is dictated by her domineering mother-in-law.May be they can't imagine that the innocent soul,now a vengeful ghost which rises from the shadows of injustice.

Driven by a relentless desire for retribution, the unborn child weaves a chilling narrative of revenge, aiming to hold accountable those who ripped her from her mother's womb.

As dark truths within the family are brought to light, the ghost's quest for justice reveals the depths of deceit, cruelty, and hidden sins.

Her actions challenge the family's very foundation, forcing them to confront their wrongdoings.

Her quest raises a profound question:

Is her pursuit of vengeance justified, or is she perpetuating a cycle of suffering?

This tale of sorrow, defiance, and supernatural justice explores the depths of maternal love, the haunting consequences of societal cruelty, and the moral complexities of retribution.

PREFACE

In the shadows of society where the prejudice and injustice resonate deeply, there was a story that explains the norms and challenges of the conscience community a tale of a women's life stolen,haunted past and heartbroken that ensued.

A young women faced the devastating truth, carried within her womb a precious life,cherished and awaiting for her child,only to be forcefully ripped away.The reason? The unborn child was destined to be a girl, a fate deemed unworthy by those who held the power to decide.What is the mistake of that child,was killed before it could even draw breath?

The sterile walls of a clinic,where decisions were made in whispers and choices by fear and expectations,the life of that unborn daughter was extinguished.But in the darkness of that tragical moment something happened.A presence lingered ,unseen but palpable-a spirit denied its chance at life,its future was stolen by someone's decision.

As the days turned to weeks and months,the community buzzed with the ordinary rhythms of existence.A spectral figure began to manifest- a ghostly apparition who looks a same of the next born child.

It wandered the familiar streets and alleyways, haunting those who had played a role in its untimely demise.The unborn child was back to sought justice in the only way left to her-in whispers that chilled the hearts of those who had chosen her fate,In subtle disturbances that disrupted the tranquility of their lives.She appeared in dreams and reflections to her family a constant reminder of their sin committed in the name of tradition and expectations to have a boy for bloodline...

Women who had faced similar choices, whose voice was muted because of society norms,found courage in the presence of this spectral child. This is the preface to a story where the boundaries between life and death blur,where the consequences of prejudice and oppression manifest in ways of haunting.

It is a narrative that challenges us to confront our beliefs,our biases and capacity for empathy-a tale of the past haunted moment reaches out from beyond the grave to demand the justice in equalable punishment with double to the mistake for a life unjustly taken.

ACKNOWLEDGEMENTS

I extend my deepest gratitude to my sister, K.Nitya, whose exceptional pencil art has added a distinctive and beautiful dimension to this story. Her skillful and delicate renderings have not only enhanced the narrative but also infused it with a personal touch that holds great significance for me.

Thank you, K.Nitya, for your steadfast support, artistic brilliance, and for contributing your stunning pencil art to this journey.

Your work has made this story not only visually captivating but also deeply meaningful.

With heartfelt appreciation,

[Kanisetty Lakshmi Harika]

ACKNOWLEDGEMENTS

Pencil Sketch Artist-Kanisetty.Nitya

Author-Kanisetty Lakshmi Harika

Prologue

The first female doctor was "Elizabeth Blackwell, M.D.,"
from America in the early 19th century. The first female
lawyer was "Cornelia Sorabji" from Nasik in the early 18th
century. Can you guess who the next pioneering woman
might be?

She is an Egyptian "Ebers Papyrus," which contains the
first recorded evidence of an induced abortion in 1550 BCE.
Although various techniques and methods for abortion
exist today, this is the earliest documented case. This
practice spread worldwide, often as a way to alleviate the
burdens faced by women.

Some women resorted to abortion because they
couldn't face societal pressures or imagined future
difficulties. Being a woman has never been easy. Not all
fathers accept the idea of aborting a child before birth. A
woman must face societal judgment regardless of her
actions.

Throughout history, women have been denied the right
to study, work, or perform tasks traditionally done by men.
They were expected to remain silent, hidden behind
curtains when relatives visited. These rules, originating in
ancient times, persist even today.

What autonomy does a girl have? She is expected to
obey her parents until marriage, and afterward, to follow
her life partner, who should ideally share both her burdens
and joys. This narrative is not just about one woman; it
reflects the reality of many women living in such societies.

I
BIRTH & DEATH

Let's begin...

The hospital room was dimly lit, the clock ticking past 11:00 PM. Sahasra lay on the bed, slowly regaining consciousness. Her surroundings blurred as she struggled to focus on the voices of the doctor and another woman in the room.

Doctor: "Ma'am, her condition is serious. Performing an abortion at this stage is highly risky."

Lady: "What did the scan reveal? Is it a boy or a girl?"

Doctor: "It's a girl. But it's dangerous to proceed with the abortion. As a doctor, I shouldn't disclose the scan results, but I did. It's a risk for me if this gets out."

Lady: "You're worried about getting caught? Just do the abortion before she finds out."

Doctor: "But what if the father discovers it?"

Lady: "Father? Before he becomes a father, he is my son. He won't object to me."

(*Here its a conversation between the doctor and a lady ,the woman speaking with the doctor was Vasanta,who is Sahasra's mother-in-law. Vasanta held tight control over her family, including her son, Raja. Despite being a father, Raja remained subservient to his mother's wishes.*)

Sahasra, lying on the bed, heard everything. She was the mother of the unborn child and wife of Raja. As she listened, memories of her past came flooding back.

Before her marriage, Sahasra had a happy life with a loving father, caring mother, and two younger sisters. As the eldest, she helped her father with his business and took care of her sisters. When her family started looking for matches, Raja and his mother, Vasanta, came to see her. Raja's father, Ramesh, was often away on business. Despite the initial happiness, Sahasra soon realized that Raja was heavily influenced by his mother.

Months passed, and Vasanta eagerly awaited news of Sahasra's pregnancy. Harsh words from Vasanta made Sahasra doubt if she could ever conceive. Despite Raja's support, the pressure was immense. Eventually, Sahasra became pregnant, but after four months, a devastating scan revealed that the baby's health was poor, and an abortion was necessary to save Sahasra's life. This miscarriage shattered Sahasra, but she found solace in the doctor's reassurance that first pregnancies often end in miscarriage due to sudden body changes.

A few months later, Sahasra was pregnant again. This time, Vasanta insisted on having a grandson to carry on the family name. When a scan revealed it was a girl, Vasanta's true colors showed. Despite the doctor's advice to carry the pregnancy to term for health reasons, Sahasra faced immense pressure. However, she gave birth to a healthy baby girl, Nandini. Raja was overjoyed, but Vasanta was not satisfied and demanded a grandson.

After four years, Sahasra became pregnant again. This time, the pressure from Vasanta and Raja was unbearable. They performed rituals and followed superstitions, hoping for a boy.

(Superstitions can't shape a super child)

At six months, a scan revealed another girl. Back in the present, Sahasra overheard the doctor giving them two days to decide. She tried to convince Raja to keep the baby, but he was adamant about following his mother's wishes.

Two days later, Sahasra's abortion was performed. She was left to take care of Nandini, her spirit broken. Nandini, a talented five-year-old, loved dancing and art. Sahasra's joy was overshadowed by her grief. Her past happiness was replaced by constant sorrow.

Two years later, Sahasra was pregnant again, but this time the situation was even worse. She faced constant torture and neglect. The new doctor, unlike the previous one, refused to perform an abortion and threatened legal action. Sahasra found hope in this doctor's words and decided to fight for her baby.

After a difficult pregnancy, Sahasra gave birth to another girl, Deepa. Despite Vasanta's and Raja's disappointment, Sahasra was overjoyed. Deepa was a strong-willed child, and Raja eventually came to love her deeply. Nandini adored her sister, and the family dynamics began to shift.

Deepa's birth brought a strange dream to Sahasra. An old woman handed her a cloth, saying, "Take care of your baby. She is with me for now, but it's your turn to care for her." This dream gave Sahasra a sense of divine intervention and hope.

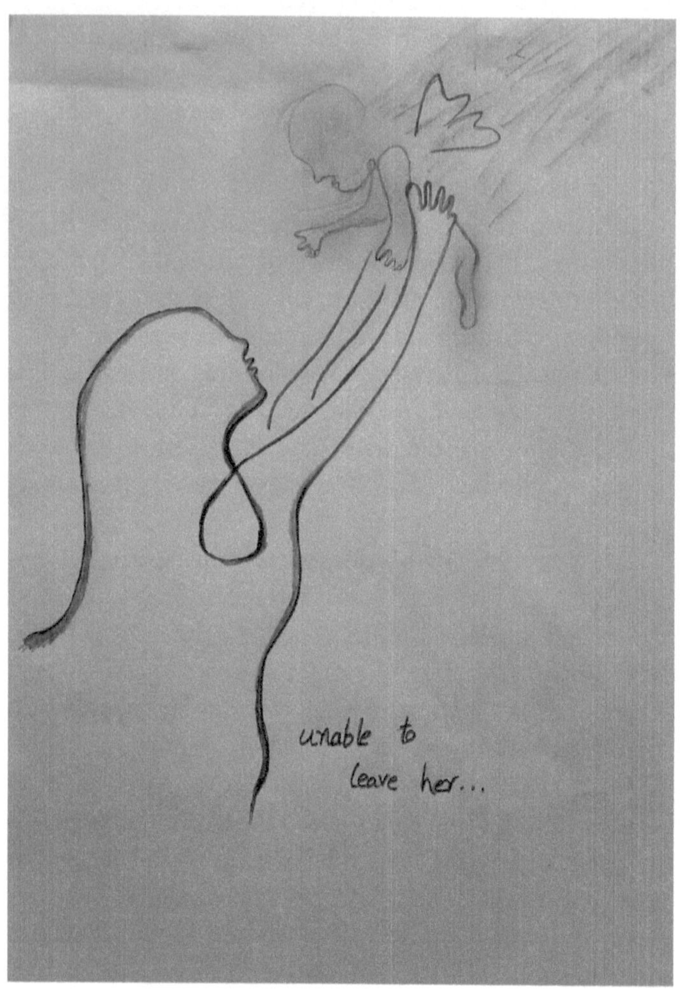

Unable to leave her

As Deepa grew, she exhibited strong, assertive behavior, especially towards men. Sahasra noticed these changes and tried to channel her energy positively. Deepa started school early to help manage her temper, and although she cried on her first day, she quickly adapted.

Raja's love for Deepa grew, and he became more involved in her upbringing. Vasanta had no choice but to accept this new dynamic. Raja openly prioritized his daughters over his mother's wishes, and the family moved to a new house.

Their new home was next to a seemingly haunted house, with rumors of it being under government control due to property disputes. One day, Deepa saw a girl in a white frock with a puppy and a doll at the top of the house. When Sahasra looked, the girl vanished. They dismissed it as a figment of their imagination.

As time passed, Sahasra's life became a testament to the struggles and resilience of women in a society that often fails to recognize their worth. She faced immense challenges but found strength in her love for her daughters. Deepa and Nandini represented the hope for a brighter future, free from the oppressive traditions of the past.

Sahasra's journey had not been easy. Her relationship with Raja had been strained by the constant interference of Vasanta. Despite his love for their daughters, Raja had initially succumbed to his mother's demands, causing a rift between him and Sahasra. It took the birth of Deepa for Raja to truly understand the value of his daughters and stand up to his mother.

Deepa's assertive nature often clashed with Vasanta's traditional views. She was a spirited child who challenged the norms, refusing to be subdued by anyone. Her fierce independence was both a blessing and a challenge for Sahasra, who had to balance nurturing Deepa's strong will with teaching her to navigate a world that was not always kind to strong-willed women.

Nandini, on the other hand, was the peacekeeper in the family. Her gentle demeanor and artistic talents brought a sense of calm and beauty to their lives. She looked up to Deepa, admiring her sister's courage, even if she didn't always understand it. The bond between the sisters was a source of strength for Sahasra, who often found herself caught between the demands of her husband, the expectations of her mother-in-law, and her own desires for her children's futures.

The move to their new house marked a turning point for the family. The house, with its haunted past and mysterious aura, became a place of new beginnings. Deepa's encounter with the girl in the white frock was a reminder that the past is never far behind, but it also signified a connection to something greater than themselves.

Sahasra often thought about the dream she had before Deepa's birth. The old woman's words echoed in her mind, providing comfort during the darkest times. She believed that Deepa was a gift, a second chance to protect and nurture a life that had once been lost. This belief gave her the strength to endure the hardships and to fight for her children's futures.

Raja's transformation was another unexpected blessing. His initial desire for a son had been driven by societal expectations and his mother's influence. But as he spent more time with his daughters, especially Deepa, he began to see the world through their eyes. His love for them grew stronger, and he started to challenge the very norms that he had once upheld. His journey was not easy, but it brought him closer to Sahasra and their daughters, creating a bond that Vasanta could no longer control.

Vasanta, meanwhile, had to come to terms with the changing dynamics in her family. Her influence waned as

Raja became more independent and assertive. The birth of Deepa, and later her assertive nature, forced Vasanta to reconsider her beliefs. While she never fully accepted Sahasra and Raja's defiance, she learned to coexist with them, recognizing that her grandchildren were the future of the family who should take care of her after Raja.

Sahasra's story is one of resilience, love, and hope. It is a testament to the strength of women who fight against the odds to create a better future for their children. Her journey, filled with pain and loss, ultimately led to a place of healing and growth. Through her daughters, Sahasra found a renewed sense of purpose and a reason to believe in the possibility of change.

Deepa and Nandini's futures were bright, filled with opportunities that Sahasra had fought hard to provide. They were the embodiment of her dreams and the carriers of her legacy. Sahasra knew that they would face their own challenges, but she also knew that they had the strength to overcome them.

As she looked at her daughters, Sahasra felt a deep sense of pride and hope. She had endured much, but in the faces of Nandini and Deepa, she saw the promise of a brighter future.

(Her story was not just her own; it was the story of all women who strive to create a better world for their children, despite the obstacles they face. It was a story of love, sacrifice, and the unbreakable bond between a mother and her children.)

II

MAA I AM BACK..

A girl seeks boat to reach her mom

Years ago,

When Deepa was just four years old, her family lived with Vasanta, whose domineering nature had always targeted Sahasra. Vasanta's harsh treatment was not confined to Sahasra alone; it extended to her daughter, Nandini. One cold night, as Nandini lay in bed, Vasanta's sharp voice cut through the silence, "This isn't your bed. You belong on the floor; that's where you deserve to sleep." Nandini, merely eleven, compiled without a word, her young mind unable to fully grasp the cruelty behind Vasanta's command. This treatment began to shape Nandini's behavior in ways that would later become evident.

One fateful day, while Deepa was absorbed in play, she approached Vasanta, asking for her attention. Vasanta, immersed in her own world, ignored the plea. Deepa wandered into the kitchen, where chaos ensued. She spilled oil and threw spice boxes around, her innocent curiosity leading to disaster.

The slippery oil caused her to fall, and chili powder from the scattered spices got into her eyes, igniting a wave of pain. Deepa's cries for help pierced the air, but Vasanta, hearing the commotion, simply turned up the TV volume, shutting out the distress.

When Sahasra arrived home and saw Deepa's condition, a wave of despair overwhelmed her. The lack of love and the state of her family drove her to the brink. She resolved to end their suffering. With a heavy heart, she sent Nandini to school and took Deepa to the railway tracks, contemplating a grim decision.

As she was about to close her eyes to the harsh reality of death, a vivid vision of Nandini flashed before her. This sudden realization ignited a fierce determination: her children needed her, and she couldn't leave them behind.

Sahasra returned home with a renewed sense of purpose, but Deepa's behavior continued to be erratic, especially when Vasanta's name was mentioned. Deepa would become irate and storm away, leaving Sahasra bewildered and anxious. Seeking clarity, Sahasra decided to take a walk. As she strolled through the dimly lit streets, she encountered a vision reminiscent of an old woman's cloth from a haunting dream.

The moment was abruptly interrupted when she saw a girl from behind who looked strikingly like Deepa. Dark clouds gathered ominously, and she called out, "Deepa, what are you doing here?" The girl vanished into the shadows, leaving Sahasra stunned and confused.

Returning home, Sahasra found her children playing peacefully, though Deepa was dressed differently. She wondered if her experiences were merely illusions or something more sinister. Desperate for answers, Sahasra confided in Raja, who dismissed her concerns as overactive imagination.

Sahasra:[her voice tinged with concern] Raja, have you noticed anything unusual about Deepa lately?

Raja:[looking bewildered] No, she seems perfectly fine. Why do you ask? You and my father have been asking me odd questions lately. It's starting to worry me.

Sahasra:[with a troubled expression]Did your father say anything specific to you?

Raja:[hesitating] Well, he mentioned feeling something unusual in the house. Given that he's been living far away for years, it's odd. He also spoke of a dream involving a hospital, but he couldn't recall much.

Sahasra: A dream about a hospital? That's peculiar. Did he mention anything else?

Raja: No, that was all. I tried to press for more details, but he ended the call abruptly and later sent a message saying he'd call back. I haven't heard from him since.

Sahasra:[her voice tense] If the unborn child is seeking revenge, it would make sense to target either Vasanta, you, or me. But why would it involve a heart stroke? Does your father have any connection to this?

Raja:Sahasra, you seem preoccupied. Is something bothering you?

Sahasra:[distracted]I'm just trying to piece everything together. There's something deeply unsettling about all of this.

Raja:[noticing Sahasra's anxiety] Oh, my mom is calling. I need to take this.

Vasanta:Raja, you need to come quickly. There's been an emergency.

Raja: What's happened, Mom?

Vasanta:Your father had a heart stroke. He's in the hospital. You must come right away.

Raja:[shocked and distressed]A heart stroke? How did this happen?

Sahasra: [her voice trembling] Raja, what's going on? Is he okay?

Raja: [urgent and anxious] We need to get to the hospital immediately. It's serious.

Deepa: Is something wrong, Maa?

Raja: Yes, your grandfather is ill and in the hospital. We need to go see him. Please take care of the house while we're gone.

Deepa: Okay, Dad.

Deepa: [to Sahasra, attempting to be reassuring] Maa, remember, to achieve success, we need to warm up properly. Just like in a game, a good warm-up is crucial for a successful outcome.

Sahasra: [distantly, lost in thought] Yes, Deepa. We'll discuss it later.

As Raja and Sahasra rushed to the hospital, Sahasra's mind was a whirlwind of thoughts. The eerie connection between Deepa's strange behavior, Raja's father's unsettling dream, and the sudden heart stroke left her with a profound sense of dread.

Sahasra grappling with the ominous possibility that the child's message of revenge was intricately linked to the heart stroke and the mounting disturbances in their lives.

"Maa i am back to take revenge"

III

SHADOWS OF REGRET

After Sahasra and Raja arrived at the hospital, they found Ramesh lying in a serious condition. Vasanta, tears streaming down her face, turned to her son Raja, "See, Raja, your father lying on that bed was so unexpected. What happened to him suddenly?"

Though deeply saddened, Raja masked his emotions to remain strong for his mother. "What did the doctor say about him?" he asked.

"They said he might wake up after some time, but there's no guarantee. They told us to wait," Vasanta replied, her voice trembling.

"Then let's wait, Ma. Nothing will happen," Raja reassured her.

Vasanta, still crying, added, "If he had a grandson, he might not have any worries about our family. Who knows what ill fate has befallen us? We didn't get a boy for our family, and my son is the last man in our bloodline."

Before Raja could respond, Vasanta continued, "If I had a grandson, everything would be different. My son is the last hope for our bloodline."

Raja, though respectful, was firm. "Ma, if I am the last man of our blood, what about my daughters? Aren't they my blood too?"

"That's not what I meant, Raja, listen..." Vasanta tried to explain.

"Enough, Ma. If you want to hurt Sahasra with this matter, we will leave. My daughters are my blood, and they are the gift of my life," Raja said, standing his ground.

"Okay, okay, leave it. You go and pay the bill," Vasanta said, dropping the argument.

As Raja left, Vasanta turned to Sahasra with bitterness. "I don't know what you did to make my son fall into your trap, but you will suffer when I get the chance."

"Mother-in-law, right now you need to take care of Uncle. He is ill. We can talk about this later," Sahasra said, maintaining her composure. She then left the room to find Raja, informing him that she needed to go home. Suddenly, they heard a noise and rushed back to the room to find that Ramesh had regained consciousness.

"What happened? Why did you have a stroke?" Sahasra asked, concerned.

Ramesh, struggling to speak, replied, "I saw someone in our house, a strange person crying and a dog barking. I went to see what was wrong, and then..."

"Dad, what did you see? Tell us, we will take care of you," Raja urged.

Ramesh slipped back into unconsciousness. The doctor explained, "Sometimes this happens due to hallucinations or dreams. Let him relax."

Sahasra, puzzled, whispered, "Uncle was always a normal person. He had no hand in my abortion. Why did this happen to him?"

"Sahasra, let's go home. The children are waiting for us," Raja suggested. Vasanta, simmering with anger, watched them leave. She resented Raja for opposing her and Sahasra for being brave enough to stand up to her.

At home, Deepa asked, "Is everything okay, Dad?"

"Yes, he's conscious now. We need to wait for some time," Raja replied.

"Yeah, we need to wait," Deepa agreed.

Sahasra turned to Nandini. "What did you guys do while we were gone, dear?"

"Nothing, Ma. I had some work, so I did it. I think Deepa was watching a movie," Nandini replied.

That night, at 10:00 p.m., Sahasra heard the same strange sound again. She checked on her sleeping children and then went to the terrace, where she encountered the same eerie presence as before.

"Why?" Sahasra asked the apparition.

"You came? I thought in anger you wouldn't come," the girl replied.

"Why would I be angry at my daughter?" Sahasra asked gently.

"Don't you want to scold me for what I did to your father-in-law?" the girl questioned.

"I just want to know why," Sahasra responded.

"To make Vasanta fear and teach him a lesson for not stopping her," the girl said.

"If you want to make her sad, you have the right. But punishing him this way, is it fair?" Sahasra asked.

"He was the mastermind behind the abortion idea. He told Vasanta about it when the doctor mentioned the scan," the girl revealed.

"Father said my mother-in-law didn't accept the baby. He said he tried but to no avail," Sahasra recalled.

"You believe that? He didn't want to have a granddaughter," the girl scoffed.

"He might have felt that way, but isn't this punishment too severe? If others wrong us, we should make them feel sorry, but killing is not the solution. If you kill them, you become like them," Sahasra reasoned.

"Should I apologize for what they did?" the girl asked angrily.

"It's not about apologizing. We should give people a chance to change. If they don't, it's up to God to decide their fate," Sahasra said calmly.

"He took everything from me without my mistake. What did I do to deserve this?" the girl cried.

"He might have taken your life, but he gave you a chance to know what you truly want. As a mother, it's my responsibility to tell you if you're making a mistake. It's up to you to listen," Sahasra said, turning to leave. The unborn child was left pondering her words.

The next day, Raja asked Vasanta, "Ma, is he okay?"

"Yes, but he should be more careful from now on. We don't know when and what will happen to him," Vasanta replied.

"Is there any help you need from me?" Raja inquired.

"Nothing, but I saw the doctor who did Sahasra's abortion. Last time they said she resigned and went somewhere, but it turns out she's a professor at a medical college," Vasanta revealed.

Raja, haunted by memories of that dark day, said, "Okay, Ma. I will call you later."

Sahasra, having overheard, asked, "Is it true?"

"Yeah, it is, but... nothing. Just leave it," Raja said, evasive.

Curiosity piqued, Sahasra decided to visit the college and meet the doctor.

"Who are you, ma'am?" the doctor asked.

"Do you remember me, doctor?" Sahasra asked.

"Sahasra... how are you?" the doctor responded, recognizing her.

"I'm good, doctor," Sahasra replied. "I heard you resigned as a doctor and are now a professor. Is it true?"

"Yes. Your abortion was the biggest regret of my life. I never made that mistake again. After seeing you in such pain, I felt like a criminal. As a doctor, birth and death are usual, but your case was different. That day, I felt like I was taking my own baby. We are mothers; we know the feeling," the doctor confessed.

"Then why did you resign?" Sahasra asked.

"I couldn't continue in that position. I needed to change my path. Now, I teach my students to be brave and not to perform abortions without the mother's consent," the doctor explained.

"Great to hear, doctor," Sahasra said.

"I'm truly sorry for not helping you then," the doctor apologized.

Sahasra smiled, accepting her apology, and left.

When she returned home, Raja asked, "Where did you go? I've been calling you for a long time."

"I went to relax my mind," Sahasra replied.

"Did you relax?" Raja asked.

"Yes, very much," Sahasra said, kissing her daughter Deepa. "Are you happy, Ma?"

"Yes, my dear," Sahasra replied, hoping her baby would make no mistakes.

Raja then informed her, "Sahasra, father is okay now. They said he will be discharged soon."

"Really? That's good," Sahasra responded.

Vasanta decided to go home for the night and return for the discharge the next day.

Later that night, in the hospital, Ramesh was lying in bed when a strong wind blew through the window. He woke up, calling, "Vasanta..."

As he got up to close the window, he slipped and fell, "Aaaah, it's paining, Vasanta..."

Alone in the room, he struggled to get up. Suddenly, he heard the same sound as before—a dog barking and a girl crying.

"Grandpa..." the girl's voice echoed.

"Who is this?" Ramesh asked, terrified.

"Grandpa..." the girl cried louder.

"Sounds similar to Deepa... dear, come here, Deepa," Ramesh called out.

"How can I come to you? You wanted me to die, remember?" the girl accused.

"Dear, what are you talking about?" Ramesh asked, confused.

"You said to Vasanta that you didn't want this burden child, that you wanted to abort her," the girl revealed.

"No, dear. It was your grandma who said that. Your mother knows I tried hard to make her accept. It's her mistake," Ramesh defended.

"Stop! Don't think I'm clueless. I know who said it," the girl shouted, crying again. "You didn't want me then, but now you want me to help you? Am I not a burden now?"

"We can talk later. Dear Deepa, please help this grandpa. My leg is paining," Ramesh pleaded.

"If you had helped me then, I

might have survived. You didn't help me before, how can I help you now?" the girl said.

"Wait, what did you say? If I helped you before? Who are you?" Ramesh asked, realization dawning.

"The one who was killed in the abortion. I'm here to take revenge and balance the mistakes," the girl declared.

"What? Please leave me," Ramesh begged.

"Why should I leave?" the girl asked coldly.

"I'm your grandpa. You should show kindness to me. Please leave me," Ramesh pleaded.

"You said you are my grandpa. Am I not your granddaughter? Why didn't you show the same kindness?" the girl retorted.

"Please... after the abortion, I regretted it every second. The fear of seeing Deepa reminded me of you. That's why I left the city to avoid it," Ramesh confessed.

"My mother said she didn't want a child who repeated others' mistakes. I won't kill you, but if you ever speak about this, you will face a big surprise from me. Got it?" the girl threatened.

"Yes, I won't open my mouth. Thank you, dear," Ramesh agreed. As the wind and eerie presence vanished, he realized he had been speaking to thin air.

The next day, Sahasra noticed Ramesh's leg injury. "Uncle, are you okay? How did you get hurt?"

"If someone was there to take care of us, this wouldn't have happened. Why can't one person stay for the night?" Vasanta complained.

"Vasanta, will you stop?" Ramesh snapped.

"I'm sorry, Uncle," Sahasra apologized.

"No, dear. I should say sorry for everything I did. I am really sorry," Ramesh said.

"Are you mad? Why are you apologizing?" Vasanta interjected.

"Stay calm. Dear Sahasra, I am sorry. Take care of your health. Don't worry about anything," Ramesh said.

"Okay, Uncle," Sahasra replied, leaving the room.

Vasanta asked, "Why did you apologize to that girl?"

Ramesh murmured, "When you face it, you will understand."

Back at home, Sahasra saw Deepa, who seemed happier than before. Sahasra, speaking to her unborn child, whispered, "Thank you for coming back into my life."

In the hospital that night, Ramesh, now in good condition, was woken by a strong wind. As he called for Vasanta, he slipped and fell, hearing the same eerie sounds. The girl's voice haunted him, reminding him of his past mistakes. Through the chilling encounter, Ramesh realized the true weight of his actions and sought forgiveness.

Unborn child being alone

IV
RAJA'S LOVE

Sahasra was tormented by the thought of who might die in her hands—her mother-in-law or her husband. The weight of death had already touched her, and now she was desperate to understand Raja's true feelings about their daughter. She was haunted by the day of her abortion, April 27th, and sought clarity from Raja about his feelings for their lost child.

As they sat together, Sahasra broached the subject with Raja:

Sahasra: "Raja, what do you think of Deepa?"

Raja: "What kind of question is that? She is my life."

Sahasra: "Can you remain the same if she were to go far away from you?"

Raja: "No, that could never happen, and it shouldn't. Don't ask me these questions."

Sahasra: "Then what about the girl who died before Deepa?"

(Raja's eyes filled with tears at the mention of the child they had lost. He was silent for a moment, struggling to compose himself before he spoke.)

Raja: "It's the biggest mistake I've made in my life, one that can't be undone."

Sahasra: "Then why did you accept your mother's wishes?"

Raja: "Sahasra, everyone has different perspectives on the same event. We often see mistakes from only one angle without understanding the reasons behind them or the regrets that follow."

Sahasra: "What do you mean?"

Raja: "My mother wanted to preserve the bloodline, while I wanted our child to be safe and happy with us. I thought there would be no regret if the child was lost. But seeing her in the hospital, struggling to live and yearning to die quickly, broke me.

I have spent every moment regretting that decision. If I could turn back time, I would defy anyone, even society, to make things right.

I loved Deepa more because she represents our child to me. I shower her with double the love and everything she desires because I see in her the daughter we lost and my deep regret."

(As Raja spoke, from behind the door, a ghostly presence listened intently. The girl, who had been haunting their lives, was overwhelmed with emotion. She was moved by Raja's genuine remorse and affection for Deepa.)

Girl: (to Snoopy) "Did you hear that? Papa said he loves me a lot."

Snoopy: (barking) "Yes."

(The girl felt conflicted. She had believed her father to be a monster, but his words revealed his deep sorrow and love. Despite her initial intentions of revenge, she could not bring herself to harm him.)

Sahasra: "What would you feel if you learned that the girl is back to take revenge on us?"

Raja: "Revenge? Why are you thinking about that?"

(*Sahasra glanced out the window and saw the girl standing in the shadows. She subtly signaled the girl to remain hidden.*)

Sahasra: "Oh, I meant if Deepa were to hear about this and seek revenge, what would we do?"

Raja: "If she wants revenge for my mistake, I am ready to face whatever comes. This life means little if it can atone for my past wrongs. I will accept whatever consequences arise."

(*The girl, hearing Raja's acceptance of her potential revenge, was touched by his sincerity. Though she harbored anger towards Vasanta, she felt conflicted about punishing Raja, who was deeply remorseful.*)

Raja's love on his child (not a pencil art)

That night, the girl could not find rest. Her mind was a whirlwind of emotions and unanswered questions. Driven by a relentless curiosity, she wanted to understand how she could enact revenge on those who had wronged her.

The faint sound of Snoopy's barking drew her attention once more. This time, however, she bypassed checking on the children—Deepa and her sister were sound asleep. Instead, she made her way directly to Terras.

As she approached the familiar spot, her heart began to pound with anticipation and dread. To her astonishment, she saw someone standing there in the same unsettling position she had witnessed before.

Her breath caught in her throat as she took in the sight. There, amidst the shadows, was Deepa—alive and moving, her presence both comforting and unnerving.

The girl's pulse raced as she observed the scene. Deepa, who had been playing and interacting with Snoopy, seemed to be a blend of joy and sorrow, laughing and crying simultaneously.

The realization hit her like a thunderbolt—Deepa, her own daughter, was somehow intertwined with the events she had been investigating. The girl's mind raced to make sense of this profound connection. Deepa was not merely a passive observer; she was deeply involved in this haunting drama.

The discovery that Deepa was connected to the supernatural events shocked the girl deeply. Though she had doubted whether it truly was Deepa or someone else, it was an unexpected twist for Sahasra to learn that her daughter was possessed.

It felt like the line between life and death had blurred, revealing a truth she hadn't expected. She had suspected Deepa's involvement but never imagined her own daughter would be at the heart of this haunting reality.

This revelation was both painful and eye-opening, leaving her overwhelmed with the complexity of her father's regrets and her own desire for revenge.As she grappled with these emotions, anxiety filled her about what would happen next.

The truth had set the stage for a dramatic confrontation, and she was left on edge, uncertain of how the unfolding events would impact her and those she cared about. She was also waiting for the answer from the unborn child, who might hold the key to all these questions.

V

MAA I AM WITH YOU

After the revelation that Deepa was intertwined with the supernatural occurrences, Sahasra found herself grappling with a torrent of questions, desperately seeking answers from the unborn child. Her mind raced, and she needed to understand the full extent of the situation:

Sahasra: "Why is Deepa connected to these supernatural events? When did this bond form? Does she know about her connection to you?"

The ghostly presence of the girl, now deeply intertwined with the life of Deepa, responded with a voice tinged with both sadness and clarity:

Girl: "You have many questions, don't you? Don't you understand why I am in this state?"

Sahasra: "So, will you kill your father?"

Maa i am with you

The girl hesitated, her voice breaking with emotion. "I once thought about it. But after hearing his words today, imagining how he would care for me and shower me with love if I were with him... I can't bring myself to harm him, even though he failed to save me.

I hope to redeem him, just as I did with you and Deepa."

Sahasra: "You can find happiness... Wait, did you say you were with me all along?"

The girl's voice softened. "How could you think I would abandon you if I was killed before even taking a breath? I stayed with you, protecting you from the shadows of those who wronged me."

Sahasra: "Why can't you reveal yourself? I am your mother. Please, let me see you."

The girl's tone grew sadder. "Why didn't you see me when I died? Vasanta took me away and said you didn't deserve to see me."

Sahasra: "I believe it's true—I don't deserve to see you. A mother who can't save her child doesn't deserve to care for her. But please, leave me and find peace. I can't bear to see you suffering alone."

The girl's voice grew resolute. "Who says I am nobody? Deepa was half of me when I died. You thought about me during your pregnancy, and now I am reborn in Deepa because she carries half of me. The remaining half seeks justice."

Sahasra: "Who else remains besides your father?"

The girl's laughter echoed softly. "Is there no one left?"

Sahasra: "That's what I need to know—who else is involved?"

The girl's response was firm. "Who else but Vasanta?"

As the conversation unfolded, Raja entered the scene, his concern evident. "Why are you both here?"

The unborn child, in Deepa's voice, quickly replied, "Papa, I was feeling bored, so I asked Mom to come outside for some fresh air."

Sahasra: "Yes, Raja, we'll come. You go and rest."

Raja expressed his concern. "How can I sleep if my princess is here? Let me tell you a bedtime story to help you sleep."

The girl's voice brightened. "Dad, it's been days since I slept next to you. Can I sleep with you tonight?"

Raja agreed, "Yesterday felt like a year for both of you. Take her to bed."

The girl responded eagerly. "Yaaah, yaah..."

Sahasra watched them with a mixture of relief and gratitude, feeling blessed for the cherished memory.

Raja tucked the girl in and turned to Sahasra. "Are you okay?"

Sahasra reassured him. "Yes, everything will be fine."

Raja noted, "But today, she seemed different. She showed sudden affection. I think she might have had a bad dream."

Sahasra: "I hope it was just a bad dream."

Raja suggested, "You seem disturbed. You should rest early."

Sahasra: "Let me check on her first."

As Sahasra went to see Deepa, she found her sleeping peacefully.

The following day, Raja received a call from his mother, Vasanta, sounding distressed. "Are you free?"

Raja replied, "Yes. Why?"

Vasanta's voice was filled with unease. "Lately, I've been feeling as though someone is watching me in the house."

Raja tried to comfort her. "Maybe it's just loneliness after Papa's death. Try not to worry about it."

Vasanta continued, "Sometimes, I hear a girl crying and a dog barking."

Raja dismissed her concerns. "It might be coming from the neighbor. Don't take it too seriously."

Vasanta agreed to monitor the situation.

Raja relayed the conversation to Sahasra. Hearing about the crying girl and barking dog alarmed her, making her fear for what might come next.

That night, Sahasra remained vigilant, waiting for any signs. She went upstairs but found nothing. As she returned to her room, she was startled by the sound of Vasanta screaming for help.

Her heart pounded with fear as she ventured to investigate, only to find an empty space. Suddenly, someone approached from behind. Her tension mounted as she turned to face Vasanta, holding a knife.

Sahasra: "What are you doing?"

Vasanta's response was chilling. "What can I do? Your daughter will kill me."

Sahasra: "My baby... so you know it's my daughter?"

Vasanta sneered. "Why wouldn't I know? After your husband's death, I discovered your daughter's existence. If I kill you, she'll die with you."

Desperate, Sahasra tried to escape, but Vasanta's knife struck her down. As Sahasra screamed, she suddenly woke up in bed, realizing it had been a nightmare.

Relieved, Sahasra saw Raja receiving a call from his mother. Vasanta was still distressed, and Ramesh, on the line, advised her to regret her past actions before things worsened. Vasanta, defensive, denied any wrongdoing, but Ramesh's words loomed ominously.

Sahasra saw Deepa, who seemed to know about the situation and smiled knowingly. Deepa said, "Grandpa, let Grandma experience what you did. You and she are a pair made in heaven; you both should share the same fate."

As the chapter closed, Sahasra was left with a profound sense of unease. The girl's desire for revenge and Vasanta's dark intentions created a looming tension.

The uncertainty of the future left readers anxiously awaiting the next chapter, wondering how the complex web of guilt, revenge, and redemption would unravel.

VI
CHANCE TO CHANGE

The next day, Raja went to his mother's house to check on his father, Ramesh, who was feeling somewhat better. As he was about to leave, Vasanta suddenly fainted while working. Alarmed, Raja and Sahasra rushed her to the hospital. Seeing his mother unconscious on the bed, Raja was deeply upset. When Vasanta regained consciousness, Raja anxiously asked, "Maa, what happened?"

Vasanta explained, "I don't know, Raja. I felt uneasy from the morning. I thought it was nothing serious, but it turned out to be worse. Who is there to help me at home? I am alone doing all the work. No worker is willing to work for us, and even your wife is not willing to help. What can I do?"

Unborn child hugging her sister

Raja responded, "Maa, the workers refuse because you overburden them. Hire them for big tasks and pay them properly. Why be greedy?"

Sahasra recalled a remark Vasanta made when they were planning to shift houses: "You guys think I will depend on you, but I can throw money at workers and make them work. I don't need your help." Remembering this, Sahasra laughed internally at Vasanta's current plight.

The doctor arrived and advised, "It's not good for her to take on so much pressure. Let her rest for a while, and we'll monitor her condition."

Raja asked, "Is there any serious issue, doctor?"

The doctor reassured him, "Nothing to worry about. She is just tense and overworked. We'll keep her under observation for a while."

Raja agreed, "Okay, doctor. As you say."

Sahasra felt no doubt about Vasanta's condition. She was sad for her husband, who was worried about his mother's illness, but also felt that Vasanta deserved this outcome. After Vasanta fell asleep from the medication, Raja went out to pay the bill. Sahasra told him she needed to go home to check on the children. Vasanta, now awake, pleaded, "Raja, don't leave me. I'm worried." But Raja went to the reception, leaving Ramesh to take care of her.

Vasanta turned to Sahasra, saying, "You didn't even give us a boy for our bloodline. At least tell your daughters to have a boy, or else they will be like you."

Sahasra calmly replied, "If their partners support them and love them, they have the right to choose. But now you need someone to help you walk and bring you food. Who will do that for you?"

Vasanta retorted, "Now you dare oppose me? Nice. You might try to steal my son, but you cannot."

Sahasra countered, "I don't want to steal your son. He has already surrendered himself to Deepa. He loves her the most."

Vasanta boasted, "If he's not with me, I have money. I can throw money at workers to take care of me. I don't need your help."

Sahasra remarked, "But you can't buy happiness with money. You can't take a single paisa with you when you die."

Vasanta angrily shouted, "Youuu... Get lost!"

After confronting Vasanta, Sahasra went home and found only Nandini there. She asked, "Nandini, where is Deepa?"

Nandini replied, "Isn't she with you? I saw her sitting in the car when you left."

Perplexed, Sahasra remembered that no one was with them when they left. She hurried back to the hospital, searching everywhere for Deepa. Raja, coming from the reception, saw her and asked, "Sahasra, what's wrong? When did you come back from home?"

Sahasra, visibly anxious, replied, "I came just now. Where is your mother?"

Raja responded, "She's in the room, probably sleeping. Why?"

Sahasra urged, "Come quickly. We need to see her."

As they approached Vasanta's room, they saw Deepa. But she wasn't Deepa. She was the unborn child, the dark entity waiting to exact her revenge. Vasanta, thinking it was Deepa, said, "Deepa, where is your mom? Never mind, help me get up. Your grandpa also went out."

The entity ignored Vasanta, humming and examining the medical equipment. Frustrated, Vasanta shouted, "Are you mad?"

The girl calmly replied, "Why do you shout at everyone? Aren't you tired of this?"

Vasanta sneered, "You are indeed Sahasra's daughter, with the same temper. That's why her life is spoiled. It's all because of her."

The girl retorted, "Is it? Didn't you say you have money to hire workers? Why bother me?"

Vasanta, now suspicious, asked, "How do you know that?"

The girl, revealing her true nature, said, "No one else can understand the pain I suffered but me."

Terrified, Vasanta asked, "Who are you?"

The girl coldly replied, "I am the child you killed. You spent your time on earth making mistakes that cannot be balanced with small punishments. Your son is coming to see you, but you don't deserve to see my parents. This is the last moment of your life. Remember, your biggest mistake was not only killing me but also making my mother suffer."

Vasanta, in panic, pleaded, "Please leave me. I want to live. I'll never make Sahasra sad again. Please leave me... my chest is in pain. Call the doctor, please."

The girl mercilessly replied, "Why should I? I don't want you to live like others."

Vasanta, desperate, asked, "What should I do to live?"

The girl commanded, "Beg me."

Vasanta, confused, asked, "Beg?"

The girl shouted, "Didn't my mother beg you for me?"

Vasanta, trembling, pleaded, "Please, Deepa dear, leave me. Help! Help!"

The girl, unmoved, said, "No matter how much you shout, no one can hear you."

Vasanta, in sheer terror, asked, "Why is your face fully black? I can't see you. Please, Deepa."

The girl screamed, "Because you killed me before I came to earth."

Vasanta, sobbing, begged, "I'm sorry. Please, please."

The girl stated, "I don't want to do anything for you. I just want my mother to be happy and not harmed by others. If you ever try to make my mom sad again, I will find you wherever you are."

Vasanta, still begging, promised, "I will not. Please leave me."

The entity left the room, and Vasanta, now paralyzed, cursed Sahasra's child, screaming, "If she were here, I would kill her!"

Ramesh returned and found Vasanta in distress. He asked, "What happened?"

Vasanta, barely able to speak, said, "I have seen..."

Ramesh, calmly, replied, "Have you seen her?"

Vasanta, in shock, asked, "How do you know?"

Ramesh answered, "It's not a good time to ask questions. You deserve what you did. Just relax."

Vasanta, crying, asked, "What should I do?"

Ramesh reassured her, "Don't worry. I won't leave you alone. As your husband, I will take care of you."

Raja and Sahasra returned and saw Vasanta's condition. They asked Ramesh what happened. He replied, "It's a panic attack. Don't worry. We'll call the doctor."

The doctor diagnosed Vasanta with sudden paralysis and promised to do their best to speed her recovery.

Raja, devastated, said, "Sorry, Maa. I should have been with you."

Sahasra, still searching for Deepa, went home. Nandini informed her, "Maa, she's sleeping in the room." Sahasra found Deepa sleeping peacefully, leaving her in a state of profound confusion and unease.

VII

I AM ESHWARI

In the past, as Vasanta lay paralyzed in the hospital bed, Raja sat beside her, tears streaming down his face. "Sorry, Maa, I wasn't there when you needed me," he cried. His voice trembling, he added, "We deserve this punishment from her hands, Maa."

Vasanta, shocked and bewildered, tried to ask, "How?"

It was then revealed that Raja already knew the unborn child was seeking revenge on them. The revelation hit Vasanta like a thunderbolt.

Meanwhile, Sahasra and Deepa were on the terrace, talking about Raja's love for Deepa. Sahasra stepped out of the room, and Raja, suspicious of Sahasra's frequent absences and doubts, followed her to the terrace. He overheard their conversation.

When Deepa cried and said, "If I were with him, I wonder how much he would love me," Raja was overcome with emotion. He joined them, hiding his tears, and later, as he slept next to Deepa, he hugged her tightly, cherishing the touch of his daughter.

From the depths of his heart, Raja spoke, "Whatever you do, we will support you. I am ready to die if it means sparing Sahasra. Kill me and my mother—we deserve it. I am grateful to die by your hands, my daughter. No other father could have this honor. I will wait for you to come back."

When his mother called, Raja intentionally reassured her, "Don't overthink, Maa. Sleep well." Then, to himself, he said, "Sorry, Maa, I have no choice. I will support my daughter."

Sahasra returned home, and Raja left, coming back late to give the child a chance to speak to her mother. Later, when they saw Deepa leaving the ICU room, Raja said, "Okay, come, let's go see."

Despite expecting her demise, Vasanta was spared, and Raja believed their fate was now in the hands of the divine.

Days later, Deepa was back to normal, but Raja was haunted by strange sounds at night. One night, he saw a girl in a white frock, resembling Deepa, in the mirror. "Are you here, my dear?" he asked. "I want to say something. I am sorry, my baby. I don't deserve to be your father."

The girl laughed and replied, "You are the best father. I am just unlucky not to be with you. But seeing you care for Deepa makes me happy. In my next life, I will come back to you. Don't send me away again. I want to feel your love and care."

Raja, overwhelmed, said, "Baby, come fast. I am waiting to hold you. I will never send you back. You are my life."

The girl responded, "Dad, I want to hug you."

Raja reached out, and though she disappeared before he could touch her, he hugged the empty air, crying out, "My dear, I love you so much. Come back to me." As he screamed, "Baby... My baby..." he realized she would return. Smiling, he saw Sahasra sleeping next to him, feeling hopeful.

Seven years later, Nandini became a gynecologist at the same hospital where her sister had died. She was staunchly against abortions. Nandini received a marriage proposal from Pavan, the son of the doctor who had once helped Sahasra.

Sahasra believed this match was orchestrated by the unborn child. Pavan, a cardiologist at the same hospital, proposed to Nandini, and they were happily married. Deepa was studying law to change societal views on women, supporting women's welfare teams, and helping single mothers.

Raja and Sahasra were proud of their daughters' achievements and their dedication to helping others. Months later, Nandini became pregnant, and everyone eagerly awaited the birth. Pavan asked, "Do you think it's a girl or a boy?"

Nandini replied, "Anything will make me happy. What about you? Do you wish for a son?"

Pavan said, "Whoever it is, they will be our mini. I am happy with anyone."

Sahasra overheard and felt reassured.

Everyone gathered around when Nandini was seven months pregnant. Deepa suggested, "Let's each write a name for the baby, and we will pick one to keep. Except for Nandini and Pavan, no one will know until it is revealed."

Sahasra felt a pang of sadness, remembering her own unborn child who died at seven and a half months. The baby's features were barely formed. In her mind, Sahasra imagined the baby as a princess, kissing her and promising to return as her grandchild.

During the name-picking ceremony, everyone wrote names on slips of paper. Deepa picked one but didn't open it. Sahasra remembered how she used to talk to her unborn child, sharing her joys and sorrows, and the name she had chosen for her.

When Nandini conceived a baby girl, everyone was excited to see the name chosen. Deepa opened the paper and announced, The name is 'ESHWARI.'

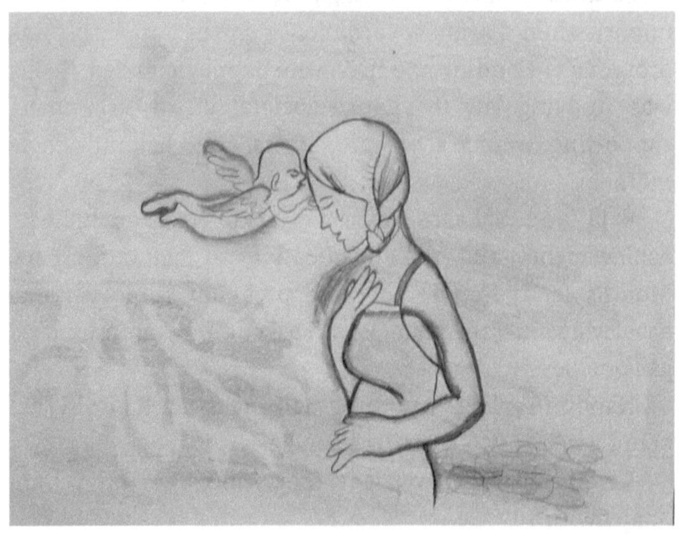

A baby with fewer features on her face kissed her mother and said, "I will come back to you." The mother, tearful, longed to be reunited with her as soon as possible.

Sahasra was shocked and overjoyed. It was the name she had wanted for her unborn child.She asked who had written it, and Pavan replied, "It was me. From the first day of Nandini's pregnancy, this name kept coming to my mind."

Sahasra thanked him, and Raja understood the significance. Deepa, now a lawyer, focused on helping women and had established an organization named

Eshwari for single mothers.

Vasanta remained paralyzed, with Ramesh taking care of her.

Eshwari's story doesn't have an ending. For every end, she finds a new beginning, fighting against those who harm baby girls and torture women.

Let's meet again...

KANISETTY.LAKSHMI HARIKA

ॐ